Body Be

Recapturing a Vision for All-age Church

Philip Mounstephen

Head of Ministry and Deputy General Director, CPAS

Kelly Martin

All-Age Adviser, CPAS

GROVE BOOKS LIMITED
RIDLEY HALL RD   CAMBRIDGE   CB3 9HU

Contents

1   All-Age Worship or All-Age Church? 3

2   Biblical Theology of the All-Age Church 5

3   'Fresh Expressions' and the All-Age Church 10

4   Dysfunctional Family: The Current Situation 14

5   A Blueprint for All-Age Church 19

6   Ways Forward 22

     Notes 27

The **Cover Illustration** is by Dona McCullagh, adapted from the Wingfinger Graphics design used for '**body beautiful?**' the CPAS conference for church leaders.

Copyright © Philip Mounstephen and Kelly Martin 2004

First Impression September 2004
ISSN 0144-171X
ISBN 1 85174 573 4

All-Age Worship or All-Age Church? 1

Forgive us if we have got this wrong, but have you picked this booklet up—or even bought it—thinking that it was a book about all-age worship?

The fact is that it is not. It is about all-age *church*. If the difference between the two is not immediately apparent, do not be alarmed. You are not alone.

The 'family service' has become a major element in the worshipping life of many churches over the last 30 or more years. CPAS, for whom we both work, produced its own liturgy for such a service back in 1968.[1] That was followed by the series of books edited by Michael Botting which contained outlines for Family Service talks, frameworks for services and suggestions for prayer.[2] Then in 1986 we were involved in producing *Church Family Worship*, a collection of liturgical material for all-age worship based on the ASB Sunday themes.[3] We have both, throughout our ministries, been fervent supporters of all-age worship—and continue to be so.

Yet we have a hesitation. All too many people—of all ages—are turned off by all-age worship. All too often people feel patronized, excluded and manipulated. One parish priest described it as, 'Worship with something to offend everyone.' That is the sad reality in many cases.

> *One parish priest described it as 'Worship with something to offend everyone'*

In part the problem lies with churches' motivation in providing all-age worship. One hears reasons such as, 'Well it helps us to reach out to the fringe,' 'It gives children an experience of church worship,' 'It is a good way of getting families in.' No doubt all are worthy aims, but it is questionable whether we should use worship as a purely pragmatic tool. While not denying worship's magnetic power, as the ultimate calling of the church, it ought surely to be an end in itself, not a means to an end (see, for example, Corinthians 14.25).

There is another fundamental problem. All-age worship fails because it is not a genuine expression of an all-age culture—a culture in which people of every age not only feel welcomed, but valued, in which they are not only served, but enabled to serve. Where there is a mismatch between the culture

Where there is a mismatch between the culture of a church and its worship, that worship will inevitably ring hollow

of a church and its worship, that worship will inevitably ring hollow. It is our conviction that that is very often the case.

The challenge then that faces us is to develop a genuine all-age culture so that all-age worship is an expression of, rather than a denial of, the culture of the church. We have to start further back from the simple 'how to' issues of worship, and address fundamental questions about the nature of Christian community. We have to build authentic and distinctively Christian community — a community which incarnates the gospel, the gospel which is good news not just for some, but for all ages.

This then is not a booklet about all-age *worship*, but about all-age *church*. It is much more about reminding us of a fundamental *value* of the church, than providing us with yet another *model* of church. When we talk about models we are talking about the particular ways in which we behave. But values are concerned with the basic beliefs which govern how we behave. We have to focus on these values first, so that we can let them shape our behaviour. Then our praxis as a church will not be accidental, but will be an expression of those values we hold most dear. We are not advocating some particular cultural expression of all-age worship ('The Family Service') that found favour in the UK towards the end of the twentieth century. We are, however, suggesting that our calling to be one body, united across the age spectrum is a prime value of the church. Underlying everything that follows is a rock solid conviction that when the people of God, of all ages, engage to-

It is much more about reminding us of a fundamental value of the church, than providing us with yet another model of church

gether in worship, ministry and outreach, when we focus not so much on all-age worship, as on all-age church, the result is a thing of beauty, a sign of the kingdom, and something that speaks powerfully of the presence of the Lord. It is to that end that we hope this booklet will help you.

Biblical Theology of the All-Age Church

2

While we might say that the all-age church is desirable, beautiful and powerful, we need to demonstrate that there is a biblical and theological imperative for it.

That imperative is rooted both in the story of Scripture and in the character of the God revealed in Scripture.

All theology starts with the nature of God. The foundational Christian understanding of God is that he is Holy Trinity, three in one. He is, in the words of John Zizioulas 'being as communion.'[4] Because God is three in one and one in three there is intimate community, a community of love at the heart of God. It is what he is. And of course what he is, his people are to be, that his character might be formed in them. 'Creating community is at the heart of the Christian theological tradition in the doctrine of the Trinity. Individualism, separateness and fragmentation give way to individuality, mutuality and belonging.'[5]

Because God the Holy Trinity is himself community, he is, throughout the narrative of Scripture, in the business of creating community. Genesis studiedly and deliberately relates the creation of man as male and female to the nature of God himself, with the distinct suggestion that the complementarity of the sexes is necessary in order fully to reflect the *imago dei* (Genesis 1.27). Being in community is essential if the divine likeness is to be fully expressed. That community expands in response to the divine injunction to *'be fruitful and increase in number'* (Genesis 1.28).

The community expands in response to the divine injunction to 'be fruitful and increase in number'

The business of creating community continues. The story of God's dealings with Abraham and his descendants which starts in Genesis 11, and continues throughout the Old Testament, focuses on his calling of a community, a covenant people—Abraham's extended family—to belong to himself, marked as his by circumcision.

And in the New Testament too God creates a covenant people—an extended family marked not by descent from Abraham, but by following Abraham in faith, sealed as his by baptism and the Holy Spirit. The abiding image at the end of Scripture is not of God in glorious lofty isolation, but surrounded by the saints at worship in heaven—a community drawn from every nation, tribe, people and language.

It should come as no surprise therefore that it is in the context of community that the work of God flourishes. Of course there are numerous examples in Scripture of God working through independent individuals. But that is the exception, not the norm. The work of God thrives and flourishes in the context of community. Paul's extended 'body' illustration in 1 Corinthians 12 is designed to demonstrate how ministry happens in the local church, and it suggests that it is in the context of community that ministry is most effectively exercised. But there is an added theological twist. The work of God thrives and flourishes in the context of community, because, Paul says, God is especially present in the context of community. This is not any body—this is the body of Christ that he is talking about, a community in which his character is being formed.

Called to Bless

The community God creates and indwells does not exist for its own sake. The calling of both old and new covenant people is to be a blessing to the whole world (and by extension to all creation). It is an inclusive vocation—to bless *all*. The covenant with Abraham and the promise to give him the land is always tied up with the vocation to be a blessing to the whole world (Genesis 12.3). And the New Testament parallel is that the gift of the Spirit, (as opposed to the land) in Acts 1 is tied up with the calling to be Jesus' witnesses to the ends of the earth.

This inclusive blessing to all comes from an inclusive community. Integral to Paul's body argument is that diversity is a hallmark of the body (as indeed it is of the Trinity), and that such diversity is essential for the effective exercise of ministry. The biblical narrative affirms repeatedly that such diversity is, amongst other things, a diversity across the ages, as he calls both the very young (such as Samuel and John) and the very old (such as Sarah and Hannah) to serve him. The community God creates by covenant is to be an inclusive community of all ages.

In the Old Testament, belonging to the covenant community began—if you were a boy—with circumcision on the eighth day. And while girls were not so marked, this emphasis on the covenant family accorded them a special status as the guardians of future generations. The sense of family vocation, through descent from Abraham, meant that children were highly valued, and the task of teaching them what it meant to belong to the covenant community was immensely important—as for instance in Deuteronomy 6.1–9. At the heart of the passage is the *shema*—the central tenet of Israel's creed—and bracketing the command (to 'love the Lord your God with all your heart mind, soul and strength') are instructions to share this creed with the younger members of the community. The command to teach the children does not come because they are *outside* the covenant community, but precisely because they belong *within* it.

This is not simply a question of including children and young people, but of valuing people across the age spectrum. Moses was in ripe old age when the Lord called and commissioned him to be the leader of his people and the instrument of their liberation. Age was no barrier to the calling and gifting of God. And of course the Old Testament—particularly Deuteronomy—is peppered with instructions to care for the widows just as the Lord does (see, for example, Deuteronomy 10.17–18).

All-age Community

Moses in old age became the leader of an all-age faith community. There is no stronger symbol of that community than the Passover, the defining mark of Israel's identity. Liberation came through the elderly Moses, and it is the youngest child who has the task of enquiring as to the significance of the *seder* ceremony. Old Testament covenant community was always an all-age community. Significantly, Joel's vision of the renewal of the covenant community is specifically an all-age vision:

> Then afterward
> I will pour out my spirit on all flesh;
> your sons and your daughters shall prophesy,
> your old men shall dream dreams,
> and your young men shall see visions.
> Even on the male and female slaves,
> in those days, I will pour out my spirit.
>
> Joel 2.28, 29

There is strong theological underpinning for all this. All must be included, because all are made in the image of God. This is neither something that one grows into nor indeed loses. It is innate, implicit in being human. It precludes age as a ground on which people might be excluded.

And as in the Old, so in the New. People of all ages are included in the sweep of God's grace that is focussed on, and in, his Son, Jesus Christ. When as a baby of just a few weeks, Jesus is presented in the temple, it is the very elderly, Simeon and Anna, who celebrate his coming and proclaim its significance. When the disciples seek to bar children access to his presence Mark tells us that Jesus 'was indignant' (*aganakteo*)—the only place in the gospels where he is so described (Mark 10.14). He insists that children are a sign of the kingdom.

Community and Kingdom

Community is central to Jesus' preaching of the kingdom.

> Jesus presents us with a dream (embodied in the group image 'kingdom of God') that is irreducibly communal, familial and social...It is a dream of a community vibrant with life, pulsating with forgiveness, loud with celebration, fruitful in mission...a substantial city whose streets bustle with life, whose buildings echo with praise, a city aglow with the glory of community.[6]

And community is central to the practice of the early church. The household unit was a crucial building block in the early Christian community, just as it was in Judaism.[7] That community was therefore as inclusive as those households. Children were part of the Christian community by virtue of being part of the family. We find whole families baptized together in Acts (Acts 16.15, 33; 18.8). Two sets of instructions are addressed to children (Ephesians 6.1; Colossians 3.20), with attendant directions for behaviour throughout the household. There is also significant material which argues that the elderly were an accepted and valued part of the community. In Acts 6 and 1 Timothy 5 the issue of appropriate care for the elderly is raised—but there is never any question but that they should be accepted and cared for. No New Testament writer argues for the inclusion of children or the elderly. They did not need to. Their presence—not their absence—was assumed.[8]

This New Testament practice is supported by New Testament theology. The incarnation is critical in our thinking about all-age community. In taking flesh, God the Son plays the role that disobedient Israel had never played. He stands for the whole nation of Israel, as the obedient child/servant which the nation has never been. He stands in solidarity, therefore, with the whole nation, in an inclusive, all embracing sense.

The incarnation also draws diverse people into the narrative of grace—such as the 'irregular' women in the Matthean genealogy, the Syro-Phoenician woman, the children which he took on his knee, the woman with the issue of blood, to name just a few. Here, God incarnate encounters face to face the marginalized and excluded. Again the incarnation is an inclusive, all embracing act.

The incarnation also demands that we take human growth and development and 'non-adulthood' seriously. Jesus did not drop out of heaven as a fully formed adult. He was born as a baby and went through the normal processes of human growth and development. This certainly precludes exclusion solely on the grounds of age.

Community and the Spirit

The theology of the Spirit also encourages us to think 'all-age.' The work of the Spirit to transform the church into Christ-likeness is an activity that happens not primarily in individuals but in community. Diversity is essential to the proper functioning of the church, and to the proper expression of Christ-likeness. Such diversity includes age diversity. Different ages have different, complementary, and valuable characteristics—so, for instance, wisdom is associated with old age, and children provide a model for the appropriate reception of the kingdom of God. So there is a sense that the full corporate growth into Christ-likeness which is the work of the Spirit is at least impaired without the particular characteristics that different ages bring.

The work of the Spirit is at least impaired without the particular characteristics that different ages bring

Christian ministry is about enabling the Christian community to fulfil its calling to be a blessing to the whole world. It is to be a community *for* all, sharing God's inclusive blessing *with* all—so building community is not separate from but intimately related to mission, the God-given mission of being a blessing to the whole world. Community and mission have to be intimately related because of who God is. God is community of love reaching out in love, and the Christian community, filled with the Spirit of God, is called to be and do likewise.

There is something powerfully missionary about all-age Christian community. The quality of a community shaped by the gospel is key for mission, because it speaks of the values of the kingdom, and speaks of the presence of the King. It stands out against the fragmentation of society, speaking of the unity that is ours in Christ. 'Where the age groups are prepared to serve each other, listen to each other, put up with styles and practices that are not their preferences—a beautiful and counter cultural model of all-age church can blossom. This model is a powerful testimony to God's love and grace working through a community of young and old, black and white, male and female.'[9] Thus the issue of building all-age church is not simply an ecclesiological issue, but is an issue for evangelism as well. In the words of Lesslie Newbigin, 'the only hermeneutic of the gospel is a congregation of men and women [and, we might add, children!] who believe it and live by it.'[10]

3 'Fresh Expressions' and the All-Age Church

We argued at the end of the last chapter that the all-age church, standing out from a fragmented society, is a powerful sign of the kingdom, and therefore highly significant for evangelism.

However, at this point we have to acknowledge that the idea of the mission potential of the church as an all-age community runs counter to much recent thought about mission. This strand in missiological thinking runs back to Donald McGavran, who advocated the 'Homogenous Unit Principle' as a key to effective mission.[11] Such thinking, which states that 'People like to become Christians without crossing racial/linguistic/class/cultural barriers'[12] lies behind much contemporary practice in mission, as well as missiological thinking—including the Church of England's recent report *Mission Shaped Church*[13] with its strong advocacy of 'fresh expressions of church,' many of which, though not all, are formed amongst specific cultural and social groups.

> *Many 'successful' churches are on closer examination considerably less integrated than they might at first appear*

At the same time many 'lively' and 'successful' churches, which may seem to be all-age communities, are on closer examination considerably less integrated than they might at first appear. John Hattam compares such churches to a beehive, with each small group (or homogenous unit) operating with relative independence in their own little cell of the honeycomb. Their fundamental policy to provide 'something for everyone' militates against the creation of genuine cross-generational community, and in effect incarnates the homogenous unit principle.[14]

McGavran's principle was essentially pragmatic and phenomenological, rather than theological. There is no doubt that pressing cultural concerns continue to lead people down this particular track. In a time of rapid cultural change in which traditional church is often widely out of touch with where most people are, it is hardly surprising that 'fresh expressions of church' emerge in an attempt to bridge the yawning cultural gulf (or that 'lively' churches continue to function in separate homogenous cells). And yet we ought to question whether, as *Mission Shaped Church* claims, 'Context should shape the church'[15] John Buckeridge expresses similar reservations: 'I am not anti youth church/youth congregations—I am pragmatic enough to recognize that often it is the best and only option…But in my opinion it is not necessarily God's plan A.'[16] The incarnation demands that we take context seriously, but are there not other prime values, including the call to be an all-age community, which ought also to play their part in shaping church?

A Missionary Approach

Amongst others, Graham Cray has given the Homogenous Unit Principle (HUP) tradition a more rigorous theological undergirding.[17] To put it bluntly, 'Missiology takes priority over ecclesiology because the gospel creates the church!' (and not *vice versa*).[18] Similarly Michael Frost and Alan Hirsch proclaim that, 'The church can no longer make excuses for non-contextualized mission. In fact the only worthwhile Christian ministry is culturally contextualized mission. It is truth ministry, but it is also understandable, believable and accessible truth.'[19] They base that claim on the fact of the incarnation, on the example of Christ and the praxis of the early church (although interestingly—harking back to McGavran—they also justify it 'because it works').[20] So is there an irresolvable tension between the twin imperatives upon the church of being both an all-age community standing out from the fragmentation of society and being a community taking shape within that culture?

One suggested way of addressing the tension is to recognize that the approach of HUP and its descendants is essentially a *missionary* approach. It is unreasonable to demand that the un-baptized and unconverted belong to an all-age community. Christian ethics cannot be applied indiscriminately to those outside the faith. On the other hand it is both reasonable and necessary to call those who have chosen to follow Christ to accept the consequences: among which is that of mixing freely with all those of whatever age who have made the same decision.

That approach may have something to offer, but the reality is probably a little more complex. A more fruitful way forward is to acknowledge that as it seeks to be faithful to its calling there are a number of paradoxes with which the church needs to grapple. Recognizing these, and living with the consequent creative tension, is far more enriching—and faithful—than simply opting for one pole of the paradox.

As it seeks to be faithful to its calling there are a number of paradoxes with which the church needs to grapple

So, for example, there is certainly a call upon the church in every age to emerge into fresh culturally appropriate expressions.[21] However, there is also a call upon the church to emerge into an all-age community. Both calls are key, both must be held together, because both are rooted in the narrative of grace.

Both calls must be held together, and neither can be ignored

Then again, there is a call on the church to be 'liquid,' shaping itself to culture. Indeed it is part of the genius of the Christian faith that it can do just that. There is no universal expression of Christian faith; it is always inculturated. In the words of Casa di Luga, 'The universal word speaks only dialect.' And yet alongside that there is clearly a call upon the church to be inclusive, provided both by its blueprint in Acts 2 (see chapter 5) and by its destiny in Revelation 7. In practical terms, therefore, inclusive all-age congregations must always heed the call to be 'liquid' to their local culture, while liquid congregations must recognize the need to reach out beyond themselves and the particularity of their own culture. Again, both calls must be held together, and neither can be ignored.

And then again, there is a call on the church to be genuinely catholic. The call to be catholic demands that the church be inclusive, embracing all regardless of age. Yet the church is also called to be apostolic. Apostolicity 'is the mark that continually presses the church to engage culture with the gospel. The church is sent into the world with a message to live and share.'[22] Again, neither call is optional, both are essential. However challenging it may be, both calls must be held together.

Reformation by Gospel and Spirit

As we consider each of these related paradoxes it may help to remember the Reformation dictum that the church is to be *semper reformanda;* continually reforming itself. Maintaining faithfulness to values which—while critical—may seem mutually exclusive is never easy. The task for church leaders is to ensure that the process of reformation, of appraisal and audit, is continual, so that we are always striving for faithfulness to these essential values.

We might also fruitfully develop Graham Cray's helpful dictum that it is 'the gospel that creates the church' and that therefore 'missiology takes priority over ecclesiology.' In saying that he sets 'fresh expressions' free to shape themselves according to culture, rather than some pre-determined ecclesiastical given.

Maintaining faithfulness to values which—while critical—may seem mutually exclusive is never easy

And yet we should also say that it is not simply the gospel but the Spirit who creates the church—and the Spirit will inevitably create community after the likeness of the community of the Trinity.[23] As with the first creation, in which God makes mankind in his own image, so it is in the new creation of the new community. But the Trinity is not a Homogenous Unit! What we may expect to find in the community which the Spirit creates are the very hallmarks of the Holy Trinity—not homogeneity, but diversity, interdependence, mutuality, complementarity,[24] and all that is implied by the idea of *perichoresis*—the very hallmarks in fact of the all-age church.[25]

It is not our contention that church should be anything other than contextual, liquid and culturally appropriate—all the things that are rightly celebrated in 'fresh expressions of church.' But it is our contention that it should also strive to be properly catholic, inclusive and all-embracing of every age. Whilst we recognize that some expressions of church will conform more closely to one set of values than the other, in the end it is only by holding on to both poles of these paradoxes that we can hope to be truly faithful and obedient. Above all, the church must be formed in the likeness of the Trinity if it is to be truly indwelt by the Lord and enabled to show forth his character.

4

Dysfunctional Family: The Current Situation

It is worth noting at this point that much of the church's new missiological fervour has been motivated by the need to react to the alarming trend of decline.

At the heart of many fresh expressions of church is a desire to respond to the current crisis facing the inherited model of church life in this country. The overwhelming statistical and anecdotal evidence of decline has resulted in paralysis in some quarters and denial in others. There has also been a new wave of energy and enthusiasm—a sort of ecclesiastical resuscitation—fuelled perhaps by panic or more optimistically by a rediscovery of the call to be a genuinely missional church.

A pragmatic response to the current crisis may prove to be the curative measure the church needs to turn the tide; it is still too early to tell. However, any reasoned analysis of the dis-ease within the church must lead us to ask what went so wrong in the first place? If fresh expressions of church merely serve to stabilize figures whilst (for example) we continue to lose thousands of children and young people from the church every year, our efforts to re-invent ourselves will have been in vain. If we learn nothing about why people have left in the first place, history is in danger of repeating itself.

If we learn nothing about why people have left in the first place, history is in danger of repeating itself

The statistical evidence highlighting decline within the church is reasonably well known. Peter Brierley points to a 'real loss' of 40% (in the 1980s and 1990s) from worshipping congregations. Even when half of these people are accounted for by their eventual transition to another church, 16% remain 'lost' to church in terms of attendance.[26]

One of the sharpest areas of decline has been amongst children and young people. The *English Church Attendance Survey* of 1998 pointed to 1,000 under 15s leaving the church in England each week. A more detailed analysis of tweenagers'[27] attitudes to church indicated that the combined factors of church irrelevance, apathy, busyness and unbelief all contribute to lack of attendance.[28] Peter Brierley explains that whereas young people are looking for a place to be listened to and make their own, church often demands that they 'fit into the existing patterns, which they find "boring" because they are outside their experience.'[29]

Stemming the Tide

Some churches have sought to stem this tide of loss by embracing new initiatives in youth and children's ministry and giving greater priority to programmes and activities for the young. The increase in the number of youth and children's workers within the employ of the church nationally has clearly made an impact. The profile of youth ministry within the church has increased significantly within the last two decades. Children's ministry is growing too. No longer is work with children confined to a traditional model of Sunday School. Whilst it is heartening to see churches aiming for excellence in specialist ministry, in many cases age-specific ministry remains the sole way that children and young people experience church and there are indications that this is part of the problem. It is interesting to reflect that the Sunday School movement, which was established to provide education for children, has now become the standard way for children to experience church.[30] It was as recently as the 1950s that Sunday Schools started to meet at the same time as morning services in response to recommendations by the British Council of Churches and the Free Church Federal Council. In an article about church policy and decline, Rachel Coupe suggests that 'the huge loss of children from the church is attributable, not just to social changes, but also to church policy.'[31] What she refers to as the 'Fifties Freefall,' (a significant loss stretching from the mid-fifties and lasting about twenty-five years) seems linked to a decision that effectively kept children separate from the worshipping life of the rest of the church.

In many cases age-specific ministry remains the sole way that children and young people experience church

Whilst Brierley acknowledges the importance of reaching the young as a peer group, the results of the *Reaching and Keeping Tweenagers* survey also indicate the potential problems of children and young people experiencing church as Sunday School or separate club.[32] If as he suggests, tweenagers are making a decision to leave the church while they are still children, 'mostly when 7 to 10 years of age'[33] it would appear that something is going wrong.

We may be providing such a poor experience of church in the form of Sunday School that by the time children reach the age of 10 (the most common leaving age) they are desperate to escape. Alternatively, it could be that the

Sunday School experience is such a positive one that when they become too old for a particular group the shock of joining a broader expression of church is too much. That the decline coincides with the policy changes of the fifties suggests it may be the latter.

The Challenge of Integration

Just improving age-specific provision for children and young people does not seem to be an adequate solution. If the integration of children and young people into the life of the wider church becomes increasingly difficult the older they get, there is a clear need to ensure that it happens earlier and that the breadth of church community experience is altogether more positive and accessible. We might want to reflect upon the challenges of fostering or adopting a teenager compared with the relative ease of integrating a baby into the life of a family and enabling it to grow naturally within the relationships of that family.

Hilborn and Bird explore this very challenge and explain:

> Youth congregations…can hardly expect to assimilate young people into wider Christian community when they reach maturity, if they keep them separate from it until that point. Young people need to experience, benefit from and contribute to intergenerational groups throughout their development.[34]

Sunday Schools and youth groups have effectively been operating under the HUP principle for decades and perhaps now we are seeing the consequences of accepting homogenous units as a valid ecclesiological form rather than just effective missiological strategy.

Not only is youth and children's ministry sometimes guilty of conspiring to annex the young from the breadth of church life, in many cases it results in a maintenance mentality within the church. For smaller churches especially the pressure to keep 'Sunday School' running results in a huge amount of volunteer time being employed in sustaining a single area of ministry. Often the quest to find leaders for youth and children's activities becomes such a burden that it overwhelms any truly outward focus. When this is replicated for all age-specific activities (including those for the elderly) a church becomes driven not by mission but by a programme of activities that absorb resources.

We need to find new ways of being church that are not so labour intensive

There is an undeniable shortage of people available to facilitate age-specific ministries whether in the traditional Sunday form or newer midweek models. The busyness of modern society is unlikely to lead to a reversal of this trend. If sustaining traditional ministries becomes a drain on the life of the church rather than something that leads to life and mission we need to find new ways of being church together that are not so labour intensive.

Our willingness to grapple with the togetherness of community life might better facilitate the true development of leadership and ministry than many age-specific models. Whilst we may try to justify age-specific ministry by claiming that it provides scope for people to use their gifts and talents, often in reality these 'ministry opportunities' are little more than the delegation of the less glamorous of tasks to the most unsuspecting of volunteers. Often the motivation owes more to guilt than calling. Real development of character and competence is lost in the busyness of 'getting the job done.'

Real development of character and competence is lost in the busyness of 'getting the job done'

All-age Ministry

A church's ability to make room for all is linked with its willingness to incorporate people not merely as spectators but as full participants in the community of faith. Releasing people into ministry and growing them into leadership requires a strategy that goes beyond allowing children to hand out service sheets and pensioning-off the elderly to the refreshment rota. The subliminal message of many of our churches suggests that ministry is for a privileged minority who happen to fit because they are the right age.

If the very young and elderly are only ever allowed to be on the receiving end of ministry rather than co-ministers in the life the church, they and the whole church will be impoverished. Investment, particularly in the emerging generation, is crucial if they are to belong and grow into the vibrant leaders the church so desperately needs. As Hilborn and Bird comment:

> ...most churches and organizations will surely find that to prepare diligently for, and with, the next generation of leaders is to make a vital investment for the future.[35]

This is evidenced where churches pay attention to the development of leaders and intentionally nurture the gifts of individuals regardless of age. A church in Nottingham works this out by mentoring a new generation of successors for each post. Members of the church who take on jobs or areas of ministry have a younger potential successor alongside.

This investment in 'every member ministry' not only has the potential to bear fruit in terms of future leadership but can also be transformational in promoting community life. One of the marks of a healthy church as cited by Robert Warren is its ability to function as a community.[36] Warren asserts that community is different from a church functioning as a club or religious organization because of the 'focus on valuing people for their own sake and for their own distinctiveness.'[37]

Whereas joining a club may just be a matter of assenting to some agreed aims, belonging to a community may take a little longer because it relies upon building relationships. However, community life and the sense of belonging is particularly appealing to modern culture. Organizational life may hold little attraction for today's society but there is a fundamental need and a growing desire to belong to community in a significant way.

It is worth noting that it is harder to leave a community than a club

So although it may be more costly to build genuine community it is worth noting that it is harder to leave a community than a club. Often the church is guilty of offering little more than club membership, particularly when what we call family life is really a collection of separate age-specific activities destined to guarantee that intergenerational relationships are never nurtured.

At best church life seems like that of a dysfunctional family. When biblical models of church life are radical because of their inherent intergenerational nature we have settled for a default position that speaks of fragmentation and broken relationships. We have become so expert in doing things apart that the very notion of being together and experiencing community life together feels like an impossibility or an anathema. However, the call of the church is to model reconciled community not as a displacement activity to avoid the real task of mission but because reconciliation lies at the very heart of mission.

A Blueprint for All-Age Church   5

So what hope is there for this 'dysfunctional family' we call church?

If we are to make progress, not only in rehabilitating the concept of all-age, but in championing it as a prime value of the church, we must let go of some of our notions of what all-age church 'looks like' and discover a fresh paradigm for it. To do so we are going to take a brief look at Acts 2.42–47.

> [42]They devoted themselves to the apostles' teaching and fellowship, to the breaking of bread and the prayers. [43]Awe came upon everyone, because many wonders and signs were being done by the apostles. [44]All who believed were together and had all things in common; [45]they would sell their possessions and goods and distribute the proceeds to all, as any had need. [46]Day by day, as they spent much time together in the temple, they broke bread at home and ate their food with glad and generous hearts, [47]praising God and having the goodwill of all the people. And day by day the Lord added to their number those who were being saved.
>
> Acts 2.42–47, NRSV

Why is this passage significant? Luke clearly has a specific interest in the Holy Spirit. This passage follows immediately on from his account of the gift of the Spirit at Pentecost, Peter's subsequent sermon, and the conversion of about three thousand people. The implication is that this is what the church formed and shaped by the Holy Spirit is supposed to look like.[38]

Stylistic considerations seem to confirm that. Commentators suggest that Luke uses a series of verses throughout the text to punctuate the story and mark significant transitions. Acts 2.41 is one of these. Thus 2.42–47 introduces a new phase in the life of the apostolic community. This passage therefore summarizes the state of the infant church post-Pentecost. And in summarizing it like this Luke seems to be offering us not only something descriptive, but something prescriptive as well. This is a church from which we should learn. This is a paradigm for us.

So what do we find here? We find of course a commitment to the four essentials of apostolic teaching, fellowship, breaking of bread and prayer. We see too the importance of the home/household for the early church.

But we can go further. At first sight, Luke appears to be describing the behaviour of a group of adults. But such a perception owes more to our early 21st century worldview than the text. This is a Jewish church—the gospel has not yet reached the Gentiles—and from all we know of the traditions of Judaism, we have to conclude that it would have been inconceivable for children, as well as the elderly, not to have been involved. While we might assume their absence, Luke assumed their presence. We need to remember too that the context for the creation of the church is an all-age context. At Pentecost Peter declared that the gift of the Holy Spirit is 'for you *and your children'* (Acts 2.39), in direct fulfilment of the prophecy of Joel that 'your sons and daughters will prophesy, your young men will see visions, your old men will dream dreams' (Acts 2.17). The portrait Luke paints is of an inclusive, all-age community in which children, young people and adults have a valued part to play.

This community displayed what we termed 'an unusual togetherness'

Our understanding of contemporary Judaism forces us to conclude that this was an inclusive all-age community. But this was also a community that stood out from its surrounding culture. It stood out not simply because of the nature of its activities (the apostles' teaching and so on) but because of the quality of life displayed, marked by the emphasis on devotion and awe, joy and generosity. In studying this passage with colleagues, we came to the conclusion that this community displayed what we termed 'an unusual togetherness' which transcended the normal barriers of wealth, class, and age.

The Essential Paradigm

Thus this passage sets for us a pattern, a paradigm of God's people in community. Traditionally there have been all kinds of justifications for a church developing some kind of all-age emphasis. Many of these have been purely pragmatic ('we will start a Family Service to reach out to the fringe and to get more children in') and often they have failed—and deserved to. But Acts 2.42–47 demonstrates that building all-age community, marked by this 'unusual togetherness,' is not a pragmatic tool but a biblical necessity. It is an essential for any church that claims to be formed by the Holy Spirit. This quality of community in the early church expresses itself in the three key areas of worship, ministry and growth—areas which *Mission Shaped Church* equates to the 'Up,' 'In' and 'Out' dimensions of the church.[39]

Worship is of the essence of this community. It is not simply an activity. There is clearly a formality to worship here. They met in the Temple; the definite article in 'the prayers' (*tais proseuchais*, v 42) may point us to the structured liturgy of the synagogue; and yet there was clearly an informality and spontaneity as well, as they broke bread in the homes. Whether formal or informal, worship was not an occasional activity, but a constant attitude of mind and heart. This was a community of all ages clearly focussed upwards on God.

The quality of care and support also makes this community stand out from the crowd. They exercise generous ministry to one another. We can perhaps detect an interesting dynamic here. The church committed themselves to 'the fellowship' (v 42), and yet we might suspect that the quality of fellowship, the depth of community, which they experienced was out of all proportion to what they might have expected. We see here a genuine reflection of the mutuality, the complementarity, the *perichoresis* of the Holy Trinity.

While the emphasis in ministry is by nature inwards, there is no sense here that this ministry is exclusive. The 'wonders and signs' we hear of in v 43 are not performed exclusively amongst the believers. This is not an exclusive community. It carries out its business before a watching world, and proves highly attractive to that world. As a genuinely integrated community it was a powerful sign of the kingdom and a magnetic attractive place to which to belong. Thus not only did they enjoy 'the goodwill of all the people' but 'day by day the Lord added to their number those who were being saved.' Growth was a natural consequence of their life together.

Growth was a natural consequence of their life together

We need to remember that all three of these dimensions find expression in and through an all-age community. In the next chapter we will look at how we can give proper all-age expression to the three dimensions in the church today. But we need to remember that it was in essence the quality of inclusive community in the early church—a community formed by the Spirit, in the likeness of the Trinity—which was the springboard for worship, ministry and growth.

6 Ways Forward

Building an all-age church is not simply a matter of adopting a fresh model of church life.

It is about addressing values and dealing with some of the assumptions of church life that ordinarily remain unchallenged. Forming an all-age community requires us to examine our worship, ministry and outreach and ask what we are willing to do differently in order that people of all ages might be welcomed and included in the breadth of church life. In this final chapter we will be exploring these three elements in turn.

Worship

The journey to become an all-age community is often hampered by our inability to acknowledge what is truly important. The failure of many attempts at all-age church can be attributed to the misconception that a worship service is the full expression of church life. Churches struggle to develop all-age services and what results is an act of worship with 'something to offend everyone'!

God's people are called to spend their whole lives in worship

A token all-age service that is not truly an expression of the life of the community is as deceptive as the facades you find on buildings in cowboy films. They give the impression of something strong, stable and inviting, yet pass through the door and you find a rather drab and hollow interior. If all-age worship does not flow naturally from the integrated life of the community it is a sham.

A starting point for true all-age worship is the recognition that worship is not confined to an hour-long selection of activities. The English word 'worship' is a rather poor expression for a host of Greek and Hebrew words that are descriptive of our response to God. God's people are called to spend their whole lives in worship, 'to present your bodies as a living sacrifice, holy and acceptable to God, which is your spiritual worship' (Romans 12.1b).

Could it be that there is more true 'worship' during post-service 'chatter' than in the formality of a service programme? Is our willingness to build relationships around the meal table more honouring to God than singing songs of praise next to people we have slighted because of their musical preferences? If we accept that at the heart of true worship is a desire to engage with God and with one another we can begin to approach all-age worship with more creativity.

The Prodigal Party is an example of one such act of worship. Planned from the starting point of helping people of all ages engage with God and one another, this ninety-minute 'programme' takes place around tables rather than rows of seats. On arrival people are met at the door by hosts and are invited to join a particular table where some introductory activities and 'nibbles' await. The event progresses with the unfolding of the parable of the prodigal son. There are things to do in small groups in order to engage with the story more fully. Drama and thought-provoking monologues add another layer of meaning. Sung worship reinforces the message and enables the focus to be truly on God and his word. A central 'installation' (a carefully arranged display of items pertinent to the story) allows people to make their own journey, alone or in small groups, through the parable discovering new meaning in (for some) familiar words. Simple liturgy invites further participation and the feast of 'finger food' reminds us all of the joy of the Father at the climax of the story. Post-meal there is the end of the story and the ongoing challenge of reconciliation and extending the welcome to those prodigals who have not yet found their way home.

At the end of the first out-working of this 'service,' there was a refreshing sense of joy. A whole church community had worshipped and learned together while getting to know one another better. No one felt cheated of 'serious' content, because the discoveries had been significant and, in some cases, profound. No one was excluded because there was the potential for people to take part in many different ways.

Doing things together and learning from one another in new ways are valid expressions of our worship

In some ways there is nothing radical about the elements of such a service. We do not need to do different things but we do need to be willing to do things differently. Perhaps the key is the acknowledgement that building relationships, doing things together and learning from one another in new ways are valid expressions of our worship as we honour God at the heart of church community.

There are those who would argue that in order for there to be any teaching of substance separate age groups are a necessity. Usually the assumption behind this attitude is that 'proper' teaching takes the format of a traditional sermon and that this is the most effective way for adults to engage with Scripture. Those unable to sit still for the duration of a twenty-five minute exposition are removed to activities that are supposedly more appropriate for their age. Of course if we were truly honest with ourselves we would admit that very few of us want to sit still during a lengthy sermon. Many of us relish the thought of fleeing to a more interactive activity where we could engage our hearts and hands as well as our heads. In our approach to teaching in the church it seems that we wholeheartedly acknowledge age differences, yet pay scant regard to learning styles, personality preferences and today's educational methods.

Ministry

If we want to be serious about all-age inclusion we can no longer hide behind the myth that teaching and ministry cannot happen when we are together. We learn in a variety of ways; a sermon, as traditionally understood, is unlikely to be the best way to reach the majority of an adult congregation. We cannot really defend alienating the vast majority of our church communities on the basis that traditional methods work for a minority.

We can no longer hide behind the myth that teaching and ministry cannot happen when we are together

All-age teaching requires investment in terms of time and skill, but should not enabling all ages to engage with Scripture *together* be a priority in the life of the church? We must start to explore new ways of teaching and learning that are challenging and accessible to all. Thankfully Christians are beginning to take a renewed interest in music and the arts and allow a breadth of media to enrich church life and our exploration of faith. We are rediscovering the power of story and recognizing the value of using our senses as we worship and learn. Resources such as the *Essence* course enable people to investigate Christian faith in a very 'touchy-feely' way.[40] As we increasingly acknowledge our need for worship and teaching that does more than just appeal to the intellect so we must recognize the potential to learn together and from one another.

The church is an outworking of the fact that God's people cannot easily journey alone. Mike Riddell comments regarding the church:

> It will be interdependent, meaning that there will be times when we rely on others to carry us and times when we will be the carriers. We will be free to contribute whatever it is we have within us, confident that there will be others who will provide to compensate for our defi-

ciencies. A Christian communal spirituality will reassure us that our lives are shared with others rather than being our exclusive domain, and that we have a place of belonging which transcends geography and culture.[41]

To this end being church *together*, regardless of age, should be a norm, not an anomaly. In order to nurture people and raise up new leaders we need strong relationships that transcend age divisions. Exploring gifts and trying out new ideas requires the security and knowledge of one another that only genuine fellowship brings. Fellowship (true *koinonia*) is not built by sitting next to someone in the context of a service but through the sharing of lives. It happens in the mundane business of life, it occurs when we eat together, it grows as we engage in tasks together. It takes place when we talk about our faith together, when we discuss ideas about the Bible together, when we pray together and when we are willing to open our lives to someone who is different from us, be that in age, race, class or gender.

Fellowship is not built by sitting next to someone in the context of a service but through the sharing of lives

Growth

Growth is both a natural outcome and an intentional activity of all-age church. In Acts 2.42–47 church growth seems almost effortless. Yet at the heart of that daily increase was an intention to get community life right — a real commitment to the things that mattered. It seems that the very quality of this community life was what ensured they enjoyed 'the favour of all the people' (Acts 2.47).

Of course, it would be ill-advised for most of our churches to rely purely on the winsomeness of our shared life in order to grow. Clearly we need to be committed to and equipped for outreach. The command to 'make them my disciples' is broad in origin; all people groups are included in the 'great commission' (Matthew 28.19). Most of our active and effective outreach is with 'people like us' therefore we need to better equip people of all ages to share their faith. Helping people to find their voices is best done in the security of community life where the sharing of personal stories is natural and encouraged. Increasingly there are published courses to help people of all ages feel confident in speaking about their faith.[42]

However, there is something powerfully 'missionary' in itself about the all-age church. The blessing that comes from being together extends beyond traditional church boundaries. Churches that are able to model radical community life, inclusive of all ages, are naturally good news for those 'outside.'

Robert Warren notes: 'Churches that are able to embrace [such] diversity are more likely to grow simply because there are more doors through which people can enter the life of the church.'[43] There is something profoundly attractive about the community life of the all-age church. Here is a community where a welcome is guaranteed, where you will fit—just look at the diversity that already exists! The statistics bear witness to this: 'Only 20 per cent of churches with no one over 45, and 13 per cent of those with no one under 45, grew in the 1990s. But 42 per cent of those with a good mix of ages were growing. Once again it proves the point, that churches that contain a wide range of different sorts of people are more likely to be flourishing today than those that do not.'[44]

Prophecy and Dreams

We need to start asking 'what can we not do together?' rather than allowing the church to operate with a separatist default position. There is no short cut to building all-age community but the investment pays dividends. How much blessing and wisdom will be missed if we deny ourselves the opportunity to learn from one another? How perilous could it be to never hear the message of a twenty-first century Samuel, or listen to the story of a modern-day faithful Simeon? When our children prophesy and our older people dream dreams (Joel 2.28), those things are to be shared.

We need one another because of our diversity and the world needs a church that knows the meaning of reconciled community. Robert Warren comments:

> Our society today is much less connected between generations. People relate more within fairly narrow age bands. The gospel calls us to reach out across those divides. Certainly, churches that do so engage are significantly more likely to be churches to which people are attracted.[45]

A purely pragmatic response to church decline would say that we should simply group like with like in order that some might be saved. Our contention is that the church of all ages is the clearest way to embody kingdom values of welcome and reconciliation in order that the whole world might be saved.

Notes

1   *Family Service* (Warwick: CPAS, 1968).

2   For example, *Teaching the Family* (Eastbourne: CPAS/Kingsway, 1973); *For All the Family* (Eastbourne: CPAS/Kingsway, 1984); *More for all the Family* (Eastbourne: CPAS/Kingsway, 1990); *Prayers for the all Family* (Eastbourne: CPAS/Kingsway, 1993); *All in the Family* (Eastbourne: CPAS/Kingsway, 1996).

3   *Church Family Worship* (London: Hodder and Stoughton, 1986).

4   John D Zizioulas, *Being as Communion: Studies in Personhood and the Church* (New York, 1985).

5   Mike Lowe, *A Church Without Walls: The Local Church—World Facing and World Affirming* (Grove Pastoral booklet P 63).

6   Brian McLaren, *The Church on the Other Side* (Grand Rapids: Zondervan, 2000).

7   This lies behind Paul's usage of 'household' as a model for the church (Eph 2.19, 1 Tim 3.15) and his argument that pastors of churches need to be competent managers of their own households (1 Tim 3.5).

8   And there is evidence of continuation of the practice of the 1st century church. Aristides, a 2nd century Athenian apologist, talking about the church of his time, writes: 'they persuade their children to become Christians, for the love they have towards them: and when they have become so, they call them without distinction brethren.' W A Strange, *Children in the Early Church* (Carlisle, 1996) p 78.

9   Editorial in *Youthwork*, March 2004.

10 Lesslie Newbigin, *The Gospel in a Pluralist Society* (London: SPCK, 1989).

11 Donald McGavran, *Bridges of God* (New York, 1955).

12 Quoted in *Mission Shaped Church* (London: Church House Publishing, 2004) p 108.

13 *ibid.*

14 This point is made in a private paper by John Hattam.

15 *Mission Shaped Church,* p 105.

16 Editorial in *Youthwork*, March 2004.

17 See *eg* Graham Cray, *Youth Congregations and the Emerging Church* (Grove Evangelism booklet Ev 57).

18 *ibid*, p 15.

19 Michael Frost and Alan Hirsch, *The Shaping of Things to Come* (Peabody, Mass: Hendrickson, 2004) p 82.

20 *ibid*, p 86.

21 The language of 'emerging church' is sometimes used as an alternative to 'fresh expressions of church.'

22 *Mission Shaped Church*, p 98.

23 *cf* Brian McLaren paraphrasing the work of Lesslie Newbigin and the Gospel and our Culture network: 'The church is by nature a missional community… but community is not merely utilitarian, a tool for mission [*contra* McGavran *et al*]. No the mission itself leads to the creation of an authentic community…*in the Spirit of Jesus Christ* (my italics). *ibid.*

24 *cf* Peter's description of the *poikalis* (variegated, multi-coloured, manifold) grace of God in 1 Peter 4.10.

25 Mutual indwelling, reciprocal interrelation, without the loss of individual identity. See too the emphasis on *perichoresis* in *Mission Shaped Church*, p 96.

26 Peter Brierley, *The Tide is Running Out* (Christian Research, 2000) p 84.

27 Tweenagers: early and pre-teens or those in early secondary education.

28 Reaching and Keeping Early Secondaries Project 2001.

29 Peter Brierley, *Reaching and Keeping Tweenagers* (Christian Research, 2002) p 105.

30 The Sunday School Movement was founded by Robert Raikes in the latter half of the 18th Century in order to provide education for children who were working in the factories during the week.

31 Rachel Coupe, 'The Fifties Free Fall,' *Quadrant Magazine* (Christian Research).

32 Peter Brierley, *Reaching and Keeping Tweenagers* (Christian Research, 2002) p 190.

33 *ibid*, p 192.

34 David Hilborn and Matt Bird, *God and the Generations* (2002) p 189.

35 *ibid*, p 177.

36 Robert Warren, *The Healthy Churches' Handbook* (2004) p 48.

37 *ibid*, p 36.

38 We have seen already, in chapter 3, that it is in the nature of the Spirit to create church in the likeness of the Trinity.

39 *Mission Shaped Church*, p 99. *Mission Shaped Church* also speaks of the catholic 'Of' dimension—represented in Acts 2 by the commitment to apostolic teaching.

40 *Essence* and *kids@essence* are courses designed to help people explore the Christian faith.

41 Mike Riddell, *Threshold of the Future* (SPCK, 1998) p 135.

42 For example CPAS produce a course called *Lost for Words* (with three tracks: adult, youth and children) aimed at helping people grow in confidence in talking about issues of faith.

43 Robert Warren, *The Healthy Churches' Handbook* (Church House Publishing, 2004) p 44.

44 Bob Jackson, *Hope for the Church* (Church House Publishing, 2002) p 88.

45 Robert Warren, *The Healthy Churches' Handbook* (Church House Publishing, 2004) p 42.